SCHOOL BUS WISDOM

Written and Illustrated
by BARRY DORSHIMER
& JANET DORSHIMER

Copyright © 2023 Barry Dorshimer and Janet Dorshimer.

All rights reserved. No part of this book may be reproduced, stored, or transmitted by any means—whether auditory, graphic, mechanical, or electronic—without written permission of both publisher and author, except in the case of brief excerpts used in critical articles and reviews. Unauthorized reproduction of any part of this work is illegal and is punishable by law.

Library of Congress Control Number: 2012900108
ISBN: 979-8-88640-517-0 (sc)
ISBN: 979-8-88640-518-7 (hc)
ISBN: 979-8-88640-519-4 (e)

Because of the dynamic nature of the Internet, any web addresses or links contained in this book may have changed since publication and may no longer be valid. The views expressed in this work are solely those of the author and do not necessarily reflect the views of the publisher, and the publisher hereby disclaims any responsibility for them.

One Galleria Blvd., Suite 1900, Metairie, LA 70001
1-888-421-2397

IN WHATEVER YOU DO,

JUST O-K, IS NOT O-K,

STRIVING FOR EXCELLENCE IS!

School Bus Wisdom

INTRODUCTION

The purpose of this Book, "SCHOOL BUS WISDOM," is to aid the new school bus driver as well as the seasoned school bus driver in keeping their attitude, skills, safety performance and their interaction with students positive, professional and sharp.

Every School Bus driver who transports a part of that precious cargo of 24 million students to and from schools across this vast nation every day, of each school year, will benefit from this book.

This book has a massive audience: every School District throughout this country as well as the contractors who serve School Districts which do not operate their own School Transportation.

School Bus Wisdom

The audience also includes Parents and Guardians of students who ride a School Bus and the combination of material would be valuable information for the students themselves.

SPECIAL THANK YOU

We offer a very Special Thanks to these individuals who encouraged Barry in this endeavor, two very good friends, Barry have had the great fortune to know, Mr. Art Fettig, and Mr. Robert Compton.

DEDICATION

I am republishing this Book in loving memory of my husband, Barry Dorshimer.

School Bus Wisdom

AUTHOR

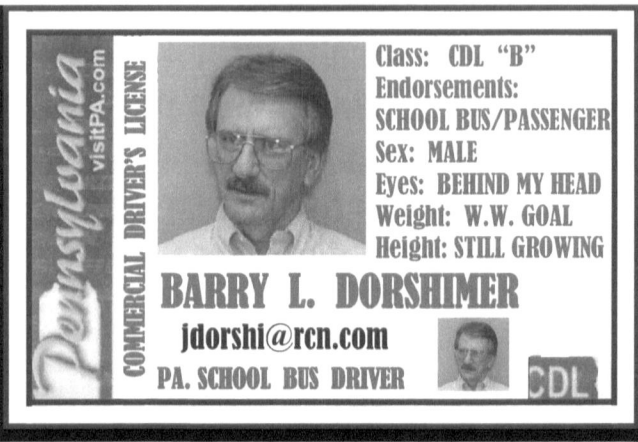

BARRY DORSHIMER drove a 40 foot, 31,000 pound, 78 passenger, yellow stretched limousine, most call a School Bus, for the Whitehall-Coplay School District in Whitehall, Pennsylvania, for 3 years, as well as for Whitehall Township's Camp Whitehall summer program.

This is a great position for retirees, who enjoy children and who want to still contribute to society and still have some free time during the day, and every summer to sample full retirement.

School Bus Wisdom

AUTHOR

In June of 2003, Barry retired from PPL Electric Utilities Corporation, in Allentown, Pennsylvania, following 37 years of service, as a designer in substation electrical drafting.

Driving sports cars, riding motorcycles and racing bicycles, piloting small single engine aircraft, volunteering as a fire truck driver, are things Barry enjoyed, so driving a School Bus became another form of transportation Barry gravitated to very quickly after retiring.

Barry had the good fortune to WIN 11 National Awards from the National Safety Council's Public Utility Section's SAFETY POSTER CONTEST from 1991 to 2002, while working at PPL Electric Utilities Corporation.

The awards were presented personally to Barry at the National Safety Council's Congress and Expositions, held each year at different locations throughout this country.

School Bus Wisdom

AUTHOR

Barry also served as the Chairperson of the PPL Electric Utilities Corporation, Safety and Health Committee at the General Office Complex in Allentown, PA., representing 66 floors including a 23 story tower.

One common thread throughout this book is SAFETY, which is absolutely relative to "School Bus Wisdom."

Unfortunately, Barry required surgery in September of 2007, to repair a detached retina in his left eye. During the 4 month period of recuperation, Barry could not drive a School Bus due to the loss of some vision in his left eye. In great anticipation of getting behind the wheel of a School Bus once again, Barry decided to write this book, to keep his mind occupied while his eye was healing.

School Bus Wisdom

AUTHOR

Following 3 additional eye surgeries, disturbing news of reality was revealed to Barry, that his eye sight would never improve enough to drive a School Bus ever again.

Therefore Barry's enjoyment of being a School Bus driver, instantly became history and it became very difficult at first for him to continue writing to complete this book.

This project became a brand new exciting and fun filled learning experience for Barry, and we hope you enjoy it, and find it useful throughout your driving or riding on a school bus.

We would like to personally thank each and every one of you for your interest in this tool, "School Bus Wisdom."

School Bus Wisdom

School Bus Wisdom

Mario Andretti's Racing School at the Las Vegas Speedway, is where Barry drove an Indianapolis Race Car to a speed of 151.02 mph. Barry is sitting in the car with his lovely wife, Janet standing by the car.

Standing by his performance modified Karmann Ghia prior to piloting the Cessna 172 Skyhawk II in the background, from Easton, PA. to Albuquerque, New Mexico and back in 36 hours, with the owner, Mr. Otto Hilgner.

Our white C5 Corvette Convertible, with a torch red interior and black ragtop, offers quite of a contrast of power, handling, and speed compared to driving a School Bus.

School Bus Wisdom

TABLE of CONTENTS

SECTION ONE:
is for School Bus Drivers

SECTION TWO:
is for Parents and Guardians of Students who ride a School Bus

School Bus Wisdom

TABLE of CONTENTS

COMBINATION of SECTION ONE & TWO:

would be useful for the students themselves

SECTION ONE:

is for School Bus Drivers

School Bus Wisdom

School Bus Wisdom

SCHOOL IS OPEN

Please don't let a few seconds make YOU take chances involving your PRECIOUS CARGO

School Bus Wisdom

SAFETY
over
TIME
can
$ave a
CHILD

School Bus Wisdom

Be the example you want students to see in this world

School Bus Wisdom

Be friendly, but not a buddy

School Bus Wisdom

Students very quickly can sense if you care about them or not

School Bus Wisdom

You have only one chance at making a first impression

School Bus Wisdom

Bad attitudes spread like a wildfire

School Bus Wisdom

Have an appropriate sense of humor

School Bus Wisdom

Always be on time

School Bus Wisdom

Girls first... it's just that simple

School Bus Wisdom

Cheer your School Team on from the side lines at sporting events, especially when YOU drive the team

School Bus Wisdom

De-energize road rage encounters, by quickly offering the right-of-way, even if it is yours

School Bus Wisdom

BEWARE
of the
DANGER ZONE

While the
"RED LIGHTS"
are Flashing

School Bus Wisdom

CONDUCT

YOURSELF

SAFELY

School Bus Wisdom

Use the 2-way radio only when necessary, since the frequencies are published

School Bus Wisdom

During wet and snowy weather, keep headlight and taillight lenses clean

School Bus Wisdom

Before backing, signal by sounding your horn

School Bus Wisdom

Be extra cautious when driving on snow and ice covered roadways

School Bus Wisdom

Always be positive

School Bus Wisdom

When DRIVING

DON'T LET THIS GO TO YOUR HEAD!

School Bus Wisdom

Keep your mirrors adjusted and clean

Smile often

School Bus Wisdom

Driving a School Bus is a privilege

School Bus Wisdom

Stay young at heart, even if you are not everywhere else

School Bus Wisdom

Just O-K is not O-K... Striving for EXCELLENCE is!!

School Bus Wisdom

You are the first person of authority students see every morning

School Bus Wisdom

☑ DRIVER'S SAFETY CHECKLIST:

☺ **Check Your ATTITUDE**

☑ **Fasten Your SEATBELTS**

☑ **Turn On Your HEADLIGHTS**

☑ **Focus on DRIVING**

School Bus Wisdom

Monitor tire wear and tire pressures

School Bus Wisdom

Look and act like a professional

School Bus Wisdom

Listen to both sides of an argument

School Bus Wisdom

CONSISTENCY
CONSISTENCY
CONSISTENCY

School Bus Wisdom

Being SAFE is better than being SORRY

School Bus Wisdom

Help celebrate Birthdays by leading off singing the Happy Birthday song

School Bus Wisdom

YOUR SAFETY REQUIRES ALWAYS STAYING CONTROL IN

School Bus Wisdom

Keep a watch for leaking fluids under the School Bus

School Bus Wisdom

No personal items on the rear deck of a pusher type School Bus, because they can become projectiles

School Bus Wisdom

Learned from experience that parachutes function only when OPENED, just like our minds

School Bus Wisdom

Keep accurate mileage reports

School Bus Wisdom

Ignoring SAFETY can result in you & your passengers experiencing an extreme makeover

School Bus Wisdom

School Bus Wisdom

Convey to students this famous quote by Jean Nidetch

School Bus Wisdom

"It's CHOICE Not Chance that determines Your DESTINY"

School Bus Wisdom

LIFE
IS
GOOD

School Bus Wisdom

In the event the gas pedal becomes stuck wide open, shift to neutral and begin to brake

School Bus Wisdom

GIVE THE KIDS A BRAKE WHEN SCHOOL's OPEN

School Bus Wisdom

Remember Re-Certification every 4 years

School Bus Wisdom

Think outside the BOX

Follow the SAFETY RULES

School Bus Wisdom

Remember your yearly physical exam

School Bus Wisdom

Volunteer to tutor students in need at your Elementary School
(it is like learning all over again)

School Bus Wisdom

Keep the School Bus clean on the inside and on the outside

School Bus Wisdom

When you park the School Bus, make sure the air brake is applied

School Bus Wisdom

Always maintain order

School Bus Wisdom

Post the School District's rules regarding the privilege of riding a School Bus
(see example - Page 67)

School Bus Wisdom

RULES on the SCHOOL BUS

1. BUS DRIVER MAY ASSIGN SEATS
2. BE COURTEOUS TO OTHERS
3. NO USE OF PROFANITY
4. DO NOT EAT OR DRINK ON THE BUS
5. VIOLENCE IS PROHIBITED
6. REMAIN IN YOUR SEATS UNTIL THE BUS FULLY COMES TO A STOP
7. NO SMOKING
8. KEEP YOUR HANDS & HEAD INSIDE THE BUS
9. DO NOT DESTROY PROPERTY
10. DO NOT DISTRACT THE DRIVER BY MISBEHAVING

School Bus Wisdom

SHIFT into SAFETY

P REOCCUPIED
R USHING
N ON-ATTENTIVE
S AFETY
L AZY

School Bus Wisdom

Make sure the roof of the School Bus is free from snow or ice, since the driver is the one responsible for snow/ice flying off

School Bus Wisdom

Neither can afford

SAFETY to have a

WEAKEST LINK

School Bus Wisdom

Don't let the fuel gauge go below half

School Bus Wisdom

Keep the windshield clean on the inside and outside as well and unobstructed

School Bus Wisdom

When a student suffers from a nose bleed or illness, have a nurse awaiting your arrival at the school

School Bus Wisdom

Have the current routes, stops & times posted in the bus with turn-by-turn instructions for substitute drivers to follow

School Bus Wisdom

Encourage students to dream BIG regarding their careers and future

School Bus Wisdom

EXPERIENCE
magnifies
COMPLACENCY

regarding
SAFETY!

School Bus Wisdom

Use your horn sparingly

School Bus Wisdom

Pre-Trip the School Bus before EVERY run

School Bus Wisdom

Post-Trip the School Bus after EVERY run and check for sleepyheads and forgotten articles and damage

School Bus Wisdom

COMMON SENSE is the Foundation of SAFETY

School Bus Wisdom

Sharing seats is a requirement

School Bus Wisdom

Regarding *SAFETY:*

It's NEVER Small Stuff!!

School Bus Wisdom

Encourage elementary students to know their home address

School Bus Wisdom

When arriving at a bus stop, check if Stop Sign and Crossarm swing out

School Bus Wisdom

Be careful to clear curbs with the right rear tire when making right hand turns

School Bus Wisdom

Bring back from vacations a small token, and raffle it off among those interested

School Bus Wisdom

Always drive defensively

School Bus Wisdom

Elementary students are often times very sensitive to correction

School Bus Wisdom

Don't lose your FOCUS on SAFE Driving

School Bus Wisdom

Problem students inherit seats up front... end of story

School Bus Wisdom

Collect forgotten lunches and personal items, and make sure they get to the rightful owner

School Bus Wisdom

Tell your students your first name and post it

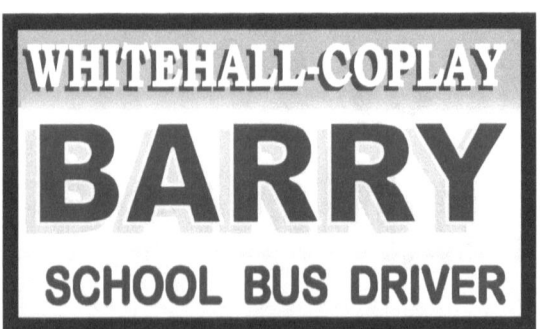

School Bus Wisdom

Correct students privately

School Bus Wisdom

Only at a golf course, can you drink and drive

School Bus Wisdom

Displaying smooth driving skills promotes a sense of security among students

School Bus Wisdom

Play the radio station students enjoy

School Bus Wisdom

Keep a close watch on students at School Bus Stops when picking up or dropping off

School Bus Wisdom

Most students are currently dealing with some kind of problem or issue

School Bus Wisdom

TIME
for
SAFETY
is a
Good
INVE$TMENT

School Bus Wisdom

Don't tailgate

School Bus Wisdom

Watch your gauges

School Bus Wisdom

Keep in mind, how precious your cargo is to their families

School Bus Wisdom

Show courtesy and respect to the transportation coordinator

School Bus Wisdom

Report any damage to your School Bus, regardless if you or someone else caused it

School Bus Wisdom

Assertive discipline creates a positive environment

School Bus Wisdom

Make sure windshield wiper blades are good and wiping properly

School Bus Wisdom

Knowledge and Wisdom without applying it is worthless

School Bus Wisdom

NEVER cross a Rail Road Crossing when lights are flashing and bar is down

School Bus Wisdom

Do NOT apply a band aid to a student due to liability issues

School Bus Wisdom

Driving UNFOCUSED & IMPATIENT has similar effects to Driving Under Influence

School Bus Wisdom

Smile often

School Bus Wisdom

Sweep out the School Bus and empty the trash containers as needed

School Bus Wisdom

Check the condition of the seats for wear, tears, and cuts as well as for graffiti

School Bus Wisdom

Look ahead for railroad crossings in unfamiliar territory

School Bus Wisdom

Get to know your students by their first name

School Bus Wisdom

Signal before making ALL turns and lane changes…… NO exceptions

School Bus Wisdom

Don't REACT, BUT ACT

SAFELY

School Bus Wisdom

It is rewarding when young students stop to say HELLO when they see you at the mall or restaurant

School Bus Wisdom

Be ready to tie the shoe laces on little one's shoes

School Bus Wisdom

Remind students that their behavior is being caught on tape

School Bus Wisdom

Submit required forms on time

School Bus Wisdom

Know your bus routes and stops without hesitation

School Bus Wisdom

Drive within the posted speed limits

School Bus Wisdom

While trying to stay ON TIME, Keep Your Eyes Wide-Open for SAFETY HAZARDS!

School Bus Wisdom

Your attitude determines your altitude

School Bus Wisdom

Never display an overuse of authority

School Bus Wisdom

Always have tissues readily available for tears or runny noses

School Bus Wisdom

When driving in construction areas activate your four-way emergency flashers

School Bus Wisdom

Have a co-worker check your brake lights are functioning

School Bus Wisdom

Keep an accurate count of students on board at all times in the event of an emergency

School Bus Wisdom

Make sure state inspection stickers are current and valid

School Bus Wisdom

Assist students depart the School Bus from the emergency exits during an evacuation drill

School Bus Wisdom

Students need understanding especially when they do not deserve it

School Bus Wisdom

School Bus Wisdom

LIFE
IS
GOOD

School Bus Wisdom

After a sporting event, mud and dirt can easily be tracked into the School Bus, just sweep it out

School Bus Wisdom

Greet students with a GOOD MORNING, even if it is not

School Bus Wisdom

Lend a listening ear to a troubled student if necessary

School Bus Wisdom

Report accurate numbers of your cargo

School Bus Wisdom

Only at a drive-in movie, can you sleep at the wheel

School Bus Wisdom

Wisdom only comes to those who desire it

School Bus Wisdom

Stay COOL regardless what happens

School Bus Wisdom

Notify School Bus maintenance immediately of any problem you encounter with the School Bus

School Bus Wisdom

HURRYING
is the
DEADLY LURE
to make YOU
take a
SAFE✚Y
shortcut

School Bus Wisdom

Share with other drivers and the transportation coordinator any road hazards or conditions you encounter

School Bus Wisdom

Never correct in anger

School Bus Wisdom

Assure ALL umbrellas are closed before boarding the School Bus and kept closed

School Bus Wisdom

Don't just offer students good advice, offer them good memories

School Bus Wisdom

Watch your language

School Bus Wisdom

Calm down an ill student and talk about their favorite pastime, to change their thoughts

School Bus Wisdom

Be respectful to ALL of your students

School Bus Wisdom

SAFETY is the TOOL to keep everyone from *GETTING HURT*

School Bus Wisdom

24 million students ride a School Bus every day

(per National Safety Council)

School Bus Wisdom

Listen to weather reports and traffic reports

School Bus Wisdom

Make sure the fire extinguisher, warning triangles, and first aid kit are properly stowed

School Bus Wisdom

A
MERGER
which benefits every company is a Merger with
SAFETY

School Bus Wisdom

Many INJURIES are NOT Accidents

School Bus Wisdom

Always take the School Bus keys with you when you turn off the engine

School Bus Wisdom

On conduct reports only document the facts

School Bus Wisdom

Keep an eye on the rear view mirrors as well as on the passengers

School Bus Wisdom

Over 90% of all accidents are caused by poor driving

School Bus Wisdom

You are never too OLD to be Reminded about

SAFETY

School Bus Wisdom

Show courtesy to ALL other School Bus Drivers

School Bus Wisdom

View your students as if they were your own children or grandchildren

School Bus Wisdom

Don't YOU Downsize SAFETY

School Bus Wisdom

Display your driving skills by competing in a local School Bus SAFETY COMPETITION

(formerly called SCHOOL BUS RODEO)

School Bus Wisdom

Be well rested

School Bus Wisdom

Join a School Bus Driver's union or association if available

(I served as Vice-President of the Whitehall-Coplay School Bus Drivers Association)

School Bus Wisdom

Fairness is important to every student

School Bus Wisdom

Always be appreciative

School Bus Wisdom

Do Your Actions MEASURE uP

to the Applicable SAFETY RULES?

School Bus Wisdom

Keep a safe distance between YOU and other vehicles

School Bus Wisdom

Check your mirror blind spots that can not reflect to you

School Bus Wisdom

Never lose -- your COOL -- suppress your emotions

School Bus Wisdom

Be a peacemaker

School Bus Wisdom

Never display favoritism

School Bus Wisdom

IMAGINE
if everyone
DISREGARDED
SAFETY

School Bus Wisdom

Make sure owner's card and insurance cards are current and valid

School Bus Wisdom

Make sure first aid kit has enough supplies

School Bus Wisdom

Check School Bus fluid levels if applicable

School Bus Wisdom

NEAR MISSES offer OPPORTUNITES to eliminate conditions that may put other DRIVERS at RISK!

School Bus Wisdom

DURING A REAL EMERGENCY Don't Hesitate: EVACUATE!

School Bus Wisdom

In the event of an accident:

Keep ALL the students calm

School Bus Wisdom

Immediately inform the transportation coordinator and request any help necessary

School Bus Wisdom

SAFETY
offers
LIBERTY
from
ACCIDENTS
for All
SCHOOL BUS
STUDENTS

School Bus Wisdom

Use a disinfecting spray throughout the School Bus occasionally during the cold and flu seasons

School Bus Wisdom

Be enthusiastic

School Bus Wisdom

Beware of any changes in your health, that would impair your driving skills

School Bus Wisdom

Never touch or strike a student

School Bus Wisdom

WHO IS RESPONSIBLE FOR YOUR SAFETY?

A. YOUR EMPLOYER
B. YOUR SUPERVISOR
C. YOUR CO-WORKERS
D. Y - O - U

FINAL ANSWER?

D. Y-O-U is correct

School Bus Wisdom

At the end of the year, take a survey from your cargo what satisfied them and what could be improved

School Bus Wisdom

Make sure you have these (4) items with you at all times:

1) CDL photo license, (2) School Bus driver's license, (3) physical exam card, and (4) certification of completion card

School Bus Wisdom

Write up a student who disregards the rules with an attitude of enjoying it

School Bus Wisdom

Compliment students when they do things right

School Bus Wisdom

On the last day of school request ALL students, that if they see YOU anywhere over the summer, to please wave with ALL 5 of their fingers

School Bus Wisdom

Some benefits of being a School Bus Driver: lots of early dismissals, snow and ice equals no school, decent pay and the summers off

School Bus Wisdom

Thanks to the efforts of ALL the <u>SAFE</u> School <u>Bus</u> Drivers throughout this great nation

Statistics on the next page per National Safety Council

School Bus Wisdom

How SAFE is traveling on a School Bus?

1) 172 times SAFER than traveling in your family car
2) 8 times SAFER than traveling on a passenger train
3) 4 times SAFER than traveling on a transit bus
4) 8 times SAFER than traveling on a scheduled airline

School Bus Wisdom

SECTION TWO:

is for Parents and Guardians of students who ride a School Bus

School Bus Wisdom

School Bus Wisdom

Explain the importance of NOT distracting the School Bus driver when driving

School Bus Wisdom

Students should be at their assigned bus stop about 5 to 10 minutes early

School Bus Wisdom

Well rested students perform better

School Bus Wisdom

Assure NO pushing or shoving occurs at the Bus Stop, especially when the School Bus is approaching

School Bus Wisdom

Encourage students to do their very best

School Bus Wisdom

Teach the importance of behaving

School Bus Wisdom

Teach younger students their home address in the event they get on the wrong bus on their way home

School Bus Wisdom

Teach the importance of cooperation

School Bus Wisdom

Eating or drinking is NOT allowed on a School Bus

School Bus Wisdom

Use trash cans on the School Bus when necessary

School Bus Wisdom

Remind younger students to remain in their seats on a School Bus until it comes to a complete stop

School Bus Wisdom

NO fighting on a School Bus EVER

School Bus Wisdom

Peer pressure can change a student's behavior and attitude

School Bus Wisdom

Any problems with a School Bus driver, make a formal complaint with the Transportation Coordinator

School Bus Wisdom

Be extra careful at School Bus stops during wet, icy and snowy conditions

School Bus Wisdom

An investment in education pays the best dividends

School Bus Wisdom

If a younger student is not on their assigned School Bus on the return home, the driver will help locate them

School Bus Wisdom

No large science projects are allowed on the School Bus

School Bus Wisdom

Remind students to be careful when evacuating the School Bus during emergency drills

School Bus Wisdom

Umbrellas are to be kept in the closed position on a School Bus

School Bus Wisdom

Be polite to the School Bus driver

School Bus Wisdom

Help make your children's experience on a School Bus a pleasant one

School Bus Wisdom

SCHOOL BUS
TRAVELS

The School Bus is expected to be at
each stop promptly on time,
and taken for granted by many
without even costing a thin dime.

Savor those rides to and from school
and the friendships you made along
the way,
your brilliant future awaits you,
thanks to your SAFE School Bus
rides each and every day.

by BARRY DORSHIMER

School Bus Wisdom

If you enjoyed this book and if it helped you even in a very small way please let me know: jdorshi@rcn.com

THE END

www.ingramcontent.com/pod-product-compliance
Lightning Source LLC
LaVergne TN
LVHW041923070526
838199LV00051BA/2708